The Interpreter's Big Book of Disasters

Edited by Pamela Murray, Calvert Martin,
and André Y. Laurin

Illustrated by Allison Roberts

The Interpreter's Big Book of Disasters

For more information, contact
Interpretation Canada
c/o Kerry Wood Nature Centre
6300 45th Avenue
Red Deer, Alberta, T4N 3M4
Canada

Published by Interpretation Canada
100% of the proceeds of this book go to Interpretation Canada's programs to directly support heritage interpreters.

Library and Archives Canada Cataloguing in Publication

The interpreter's big book of disasters / edited by Pamela Murray, Calvert Martin, and André Y. Laurin ; illustrated by Allison Roberts.

Issued in print and electronic formats.
ISBN 978-0-9947591-0-8 (paperback).--ISBN 978-0-9947591-1-5 (kindle)

1. Interpretation of cultural and natural resources--Canada--Humor.
2. Interpretation of cultural and natural resources--United States--Humor.
I. Murray, Pamela, 1974-, editor II. Laurin, André Y., 1980-, editor
III. Martin, Calvert, 1974-, editor IV. Roberts, Allison, 1980-, illustrator
V. Interpretation Canada, issuing body

GV181.18.I57 2015   363.6'9   C2015-904229-1
                                            C2015-904230-5

To Doug and Carol, master interpreters and beloved mentors, who were always there to help me laugh and look for lessons when programs went wrong - PM

To Jeannie, who is my love, my buddy, and my muse, and who tolerates all my crazy ideas. And, of course, to Casey and Finnegan who will always be chasing squirrels in my heart. - CM

To Kate, Sarah and Émilie (and baby 3.0), who support my addiction to nature and allow me to share my love of interpretation with them on family hikes (read as holding them back on the trail to talk about lichen or worms!) - AYL

Acknowledgements

Creating this book was an exciting adventure for all of us. We are especially inspired because the entire book is the result of voluntary contributions from interpreters. The stories, the illustrations, the design, and the editing have all been done by interpreters, all free of charge, and all for the benefit of the interpretive community. We worked late at night, during coffee breaks, in between school programs, during commutes, and even in our sleep. You could say it is the outcome of a whole community of interpreters coming together.

In particular, we would like to thank the following:

Alli Roberts for her hilarious and inspiring illustrations. They brought our chapters to life, and the cover had us searching for all the hidden jokes and references to the stories.

Lyn Elliott for her design and layout. If it wasn't for her, you would be holding a bunch of photocopied sheets stapled together.

Of course this book would not be possible without the willingness of numerous authors to share their talented writing and life experience with us. Their names are (in alphabetical order): Paul Bruneau, Nicole Cann, Marisol Asselta Castro, Don Enright, Victoria Evans, Monica Field, Heather Graham-Nakaska, Paul Halychuk, Sam Ham, Margot Hervieux, Amandeep Johal, Sherry Kirkvold, Richard Kool, Scott Mair, Kathy McPherson, Kenton Otterbein, Munju Monique Ravindra, Heidi Scarfone, Peter Stobie, Greg Stroud, Sheila Wiebe, and Stephanie Yuill. We are honoured that they are all willing to share their embarrassing stories with the world.

Finally, all the past, present, and future board members and volunteers of Interpretation Canada, for keeping the professional interpretive community and sense of camaraderie alive.

Contents

To Err Is Human

Introduction

When we first came up with the idea of writing The Interpreter's Big Book of Disasters, we were only kidding. We were conducting an online meeting to brainstorm ideas on how Interpretation Canada could support interpreters. It was the best kind of brainstorming, where all ideas were accepted in an effort to get to something truly brilliant:

"I know, let's make backpacks that say 'Grab Bag' on them."

"We could make them first aid kits."

"Yes! Or, what about a survival kit for interpreters? You know, with everything you need for when a program goes wrong?"

"What, like batteries and duct tape?"

"And snacks!"

"And a flask of whiskey!"

"It could have a little manual in it, like those books you get in first aid kits that tell you what to do when someone breaks their arm."

"You mean like a 'Worst Case Scenario Survival Guide' for interpreters?"

The next thing we knew, the three of us were meeting over the phone to seriously discuss the idea. We spent most of that first phone call sharing our own disaster stories. Like Pam's dramatic evening theatre program that was interrupted by a squirrel that lived in the amphitheatre stage and enjoyed running across the screen at the worst possible moments. Or Cal's dynamic talk on a cruise ship, where he discovered after 45 minutes, to his horror, that the large crowd didn't even speak English and was only there to listen to the German disembarkation instructions which followed his talk. And then there was the time André's live animal demonstration involving a porcupine went horribly awry when the lonely male porcupine fell in love with André's leg.

As the stories began to flow, we soon realized that these types of interpretive disasters have happened to all of us. From an urban interpreter accidentally leading a walking tour into the middle of drug deal, to a misspoken word in a puppet show causing uncontrollable laughter, it seems that every interpreter has at least one story to share.

There is a wonderful kind of catharsis in sharing our failures with our colleagues. Telling these stories helps us realize that we are not alone in having made mistakes. Plus, the supportive chuckles of laughter when other interpreters recognize themselves in our stories draw us closer together as a professional community.

The biggest reason we decided this book needed to be created, however, was that these disaster stories are powerful learning tools. Mistakes are humbling, but they are also incredibly effective teachers. If you find a washed out bridge in the middle of a guided hike and have to explain why you are turning around to a group of confused visitors, you may feel awful, but you will also never again forget to check the trail report before setting out. It is even better, though, if you can read a story where another interpreter encounters a washed out bridge, so you can learn the importance of checking the trail report without having to make the mistake yourself.

Thanks to the brave interpreters from across North America who shared their stories with us, we are able to present an entire book full of valuable experiences. We hope that this book will save you from a few disasters of your own, and perhaps cause some supportive chuckles of laughter as you read it.

Pamela Murray, Calvert Martin, and André Y. Laurin
Fall 2015

Nature Unleashed
Animals and Weather

The unpredictability of the natural world can make ordinary interpretive programs absolutely magical... and can completely ruin them. From aggressive animals to sudden rainstorms, these stories come from interpreters who have weathered the worst nature has to offer.

Attack Turtle

Disaster Zone: Royal Botanical Gardens Nature Centre, Burlington, Ontario

Heidi Scarfone, Nature Interpreter
Royal Botanical Gardens, Burlington, Ontario

We have four species of turtle at the nature centre where I work. Three are native species and one is definitely an "alien." Chompers, as I have now renamed him, is a red-eared slider, commonly found in the southern United States and sold by many pet stores.

Chompers was found in one of the ponds on the nature centre property. He was most likely placed there by some well-meaning person who didn't want to keep him, but also didn't want to flush him down the toilet, so instead took him on a road trip and left him in his new home.

He was cute and small when he arrived, so we added him to our turtle tank. He made new friends, despite being a bit of a bully to the local painted turtles.

We use the turtles to educate school children and visitors. We often deliver "turtle talks" which involve taking a turtle out of its tank, but not every turtle is right for the program. We leave Geronimo in HIS tank because he is a huge snapper ....need I say more?

I was experienced in handling the gentle Blanding's turtle, Bea, as well as the painted turtles. But, I had never used Chompers because he was relatively new to the tank.

One day, a visiting family wanted to see the turtles up close and personal. So, I decided to bring out the "little" red-eared slider to strut his stuff.

With the family gathered around me on the carpeted floor, I introduced them to my sweet shelled friend. The kids were so excited and their eyes widened as I began to show them different parts of the turtle, starting with the shape of its shell. Just as I was about to show them his front feet and nails, he quickly attached himself to my finger.

I was shocked and tried to remain calm as the family looked on in horror. I figured that because this turtle was so small, it shouldn't take much to get him off of my finger. But, the more I pulled, the harder his beaked grip became. Trying not to screech (it really started to hurt!), I continued to talk about the turtle. I mentioned that it is probably a good idea to keep one's fingers away from a turtle's mouth and pointed out that if I had been a passing minnow, the turtle is well equipped to trap food in its sharp mouth.

For some reason, at that point, one of the kids decided to ask me where the turtle's vagina was! Great. Here I am trying to get a red-eared slider off of my finger and the kid wants to know where the turtle's reproductive organs are.

"Well, I am not really sure." (I didn't know how to determine the sex of a turtle and wasn't sure if it even had a vagina!)

"Do you know where its penis is?"

Keep in mind, the turtle is still attached to my finger and not showing any signs of letting go!

"Well, that is a really good question. How about we talk about the shell of the turtle right now while I try and get it off of my finger?"

Of course, the other children were all laughing, probably because the turtle was now a hand accessory, and also because the kid had said two words that most children find funny!

"I want to see the turtle's vagina and penis," the little boy kept repeating.

Chompers began to release his tight grip, but as I started to move my finger he quickly tightened it up again.

Thankfully, the boy's father reigned him in and tried to redirect his questions to other anatomical parts of the shelled tiger.

It seemed to take forever before the turtle let go, and he was quickly returned to his tank after a stern talking to. The kids followed me and became interested in Geronimo, wanting me to take him out of his tank. Yeah, right!

We settled on taking out the Blanding's turtle and enjoyed the rest of the program without any more discussion about the turtle's sexy parts or anyone getting attached to its mouth.

What would I do if I could go back in time? Probably hang the CLOSED sign on the door of the nature centre! Haha!

I guess that I would have familiarized myself with the red-eared slider before handling him in public. I would have found out that he was vicious and handled him accordingly, making sure that my finger was as far away from his mouth as possible, holding him by the rear of his shell.

I have since learned that it is difficult to determine the sex of this type of turtle when it is young and that turtles do, in fact, have a penis (if male) and the females have a cloaca. Phew…

Ogden Nash verse:

The turtle lives 'twixt plated decks

That practically conceal its sex.

I think it clever of the turtle

In such a fix to be so fertile.

Editors' Tips

When faced with an awkward question from the audience:

- Be professional and always encourage a sense of wonder. They may not realize it is an awkward question.

- It's okay to defer the question to another person or another time, if appropriate.

- Remember this story and be grateful that there isn't a turtle biting your hand as well.

Cleavage Squirrel

Disaster Zone: Science North, Sudbury, Ontario

André Laurin, Interpretation Coordinator
Prince Edward Island National Park, Prince Edward Island

Live animal demonstrations are a hoot, especially when your furry colleague is unpredictable and things go wild. My sidekicks on this particular demonstration were Sabrina and Dale, two "seasoned" Northern flying squirrels that had been hand-raised by staff in the Biosphere at Science North, where a series of habitat enclosures showcased the fauna of Northern Ontario. These animal ambassadors demonstrated their gliding skills during live demonstrations by jumping off of a science demonstrator's hand, gliding down a few meters and landing on another demonstrator who was wearing a lab coat, only to disappear into one of coat's pockets. Science demonstrators were, and still are, referred to as "Bluecoats" after their distinctive blue lab coats, the pockets of which were like second homes for the squirrels.

My assistant was a new student volunteer who had observed, but never participated in this demonstration. The crowd was a typical gathering of about 100 visitors composed mainly of families with children of various ages. The time arrived in the demonstration when the squirrels would do their thing.

Typically, I would get Dale to show-off first, because he was unpredictable in his willingness to jump. I often got a few chuckles from the crowd by insisting that Dale had a fear of flying. However, on this particular day, I decided to get Sabrina out of my pocket first. Standing on top of a five-foot tall fake boulder, I reached into one of my trusty lab coat pockets, pulled out Sabrina and laid her onto my outstretched hand. As expected, Sabrina dutifully located the other Bluecoat in the crowd, bobbed her head up-and-down a few times and jumped. She landed on my assistant's chest and scurried right into one of the lab coat pockets to the great amusement of the crowd. This was repeated a second time in

13

case anyone missed it.

Now came the climax of the show; someone from the crowd would be chosen to wear the blue lab coat and become a flying squirrel landing strip! As a sort of "welcome-to-the-team" initiation, I put the spotlight on my assistant to choose one lucky visitor. After some hesitation (likely due to shock), my assistant chose a mother from the crowd. The woman reluctantly agreed to participate after some encouragement from her family and put on the lab coat.

After a warm welcome and introduction, I gave her few standard instructions: tie your hair back, stand right in that spot, and don't close your eyes. I took Sabrina out of my pocket knowing that Dale might not jump. I placed the squirrel on my hand and it sat there only for an instant before jumping as though its tail was set ablaze.

Our brave volunteer let out a shrill scream of panic. Sabrina had landed on the woman's chest, and rather than scurry down into the lab coat's pocket as was expected, she made a beeline straight into the lady's bosom. My rookie assistant and I had failed to ask the volunteer, who was quite busty and wearing a V-neck shirt, to fully button-up the lab coat.

The crowd burst into hysterical laughter at the sight of this poor lady jumping up and down and screaming at the top of her lungs, "It's in my shirt! It's in my shirt!" I jumped down from my perch and attempted to calm her. When this proved useless, I asked my female assistant to take the volunteer to a private area and help with extracting the squirrel.

Needless to say, the extraction is fodder for another good story. Sabrina was finally removed from the volunteer, who by then had suffered scratches over various parts of her torso. There was a fanfare of applause and cheer from the crowd as she returned to her family, fully embarrassed.

It was only when Sabrina was returned to me that I realized it was Dale all along! I profusely apologized for Dale's behaviour and then hastily wrapped-up the demonstration.

To this day, I can't help but wonder why I changed my routine, or why I asked a rookie assistant to pick a volunteer without prior discussion. Most of all, I will never forget how merciful that poor lady was after having put her through such agony, nor how it felt to be stuck between a rock and a hard place!

Editors' Tips

When faced with unpredictable animal sidekicks:

- Know the individual animals and their tendencies well.

- Think through possible situations (e.g. the animal won't cooperate, it bites you, etc.) and have contingency plans in place.

- Remember to stick to your plan and play it cool when the unexpected happens (all while keeping your shirt buttoned-up, of course).

- Use humour. If it bites you say, "Oh, this happens all of the time! I just don't know why it loves me so much."

Squirting Sea Cucumber

Disaster Zone: Porlier Pass, Galiano Island, British Columbia

Richard Kool, School of Environment and Sustainability
Royal Roads University, Victoria, British Columbia

I have taken people down to the shore for decades, now. It's a selfish habit, really, because I love seeing the pleasure and excitement people feel when finding wonderful things in tidepools. And having spent most of my adult life on Vancouver Island, you really can't get better tidepools anyplace else in Canada. Low tides on the west coast of Vancouver Island are simply the best.

I feel fortunate that, through my various jobs, I've had lots of chances to let people play and learn and be inspired at the shore. The issue, for an interpreter, in taking people away from the structured setting of a campfire show or museum exhibit, is that once outside in the field, we lose the control we might have in a more organized setting.

During my first trip taking a group of first-year university students to Botanical Beach on the west coast of the island, I nearly had one washed away by a rogue wave. However, and to both of our good fortunes, the student did take to heart the warning I gave them, written in the early 1940s by the great west coast marine biologist Ed Ricketts: "It has been stated that in some regions any person within 20 feet of the water, vertically, is in constant danger of losing his life… To lie down, cling to the rocks like a seastar and let a great wave pour over one takes nerve and a cool head; but more often than not it is the only sane course of action."

Sometimes, my enthusiasm would run away with me a wee bit and cause some discomfort amongst my audience, like when I was taking a Christian high school class to the beach, and pointed out *Balanus nubilus*, the giant acorn barnacle, which I described as "the biggest F… ing barnacle in the world." This wasn't appreciated by the teachers and parents, but at least the kids did get the idea.

And, there was the time when one of the elderly Royal British Columbia Museum (RBCM) docents actually slipped into a tidepool and sat there, laughing, up to her waist in water.

One spring, I arranged to take a group of keen RBCM docents on a wonderful day-long adventure to Porlier Pass on the north end of Galiano Island. While the intertidal life around Galiano is wonderful in general, the currents sweeping up to 16 kilometers an hour through Porlier Pass seem to create conditions for an even richer diversity of marine invertebrate life.

Down on the rocks that day, I had one of my greatest disasters as an interpreter. We were finding fabulous creatures, colourful and wonderful, from many phyla. Someone spotted a huge red and spiked sea cucumber, the largest we have in coastal British Columbia, a beautiful *Parastichopus californicus* about 35-40 cm. long. The docents gathered around, waiting for one of my riveting explanations about the anatomy, physiology and ecology of this creature. While in the water, this sea cucumber has a very soft and jelly-like feel to it, but as I held it with both hands, I could feel it hardening as its sphincters closed up and its muscles tightened up. The docents were fascinated and wanted to feel this hard, red, and wet creature. Getting an up close and personal look at the beast, one of the docents, a woman who had left her middle age far behind, said "Oh My" and as her mouth formed the "Oh", the cucumber evacuated its internal water supply in a long and powerful stream from its anus into the docent's mouth.

For a moment, no one knew what to say. And so I did what all wise interpreters know to do when things don't work out as expected: I laughed, the others laughed, and once she spit the sea water out of her mouth, the docent laughed too. No harm done!

I love this little poem by ee cummings, which should be memorized by all marine interpreters!

> maggie and milly and molly and may
> went down to the beach (to play one day)
> and maggie discovered a shell that sang
> so sweetly she couldn't remember her troubles,and
> milly befriended a stranded star
> whose rays five languid fingers were;
> and molly was chased by a horrible thing

which raced sideways while blowing bubbles: and
may came home with a smooth round stone
as small as a world and as large as alone.
For whatever we lose (like a you or a me)
it's always ourselves we find in the sea.

Editors' Tips

When faced with a sudden and unexpected natural event:

- Don't ignore it. Embrace it!

- Turn it into a teachable moment. "One of the fascinating things about sea cucumbers is that some of them can expel all of their internal organs, and regrow new ones, in order to escape a predator. So this could have been much, much worse."

- Know your topic. The more familiar you are with it, the more prepared you will be for these types of occurrences.

Badlands

Disaster Zone: Dinosaur Provincial Park, Alberta

Paul Halychuk, Park Interpreter
Metro Vancouver Regional Parks, Vancouver, British Columbia

The storm hit when we were inside the hadrosaur shelter, situated on a high, exposed hill in Alberta's Dinosaur Provincial Park. Bits and pieces of dinosaurs and other prehistoric creatures are found everywhere in the park, but nearly complete skeletons like the hadrosaur are very rare. The park had built the small concrete shelter over this hadrosaur skeleton to protect it from thieves and from weather.

I was discussing what might have caused the death of this dinosaur with the two women on my tour, when a blast of sand blew through the open door. There had not been a cloud in the sky when we entered the concrete shelter around half an hour earlier. But, when I stepped outside, I discovered a great mass of dark cloud looming over us and rapidly spreading across the sky.

I looked at the large, metal doors of the small shelter. My first concern was that lightning might be attracted to the doors, so I decided that the bus was a better place to be.

My second concern was rain. The Badlands are a vast moonscape of sandstone cliffs, spires, and canyons carved down into the prairie. Sandstone absorbs water and becomes as slippery as grease when it gets wet. When it rains, you can't safely move around for hours or even days until the ground dries out.

The two women were retired teachers, a mother and daughter from New Jersey on their first trip to Western Canada. They had seemed fascinated by the hadrosaur skeleton and the fossils that we passed around, but they were definitely not outdoorsy types who would be up for a long hike out. Of the many interpretive programs at the park, seniors and less active people often choose the bus tour because it sounds like it will be the easiest on their feet.

But, that would all change if we had to hike out because the bus got stuck or the roads washed out. Our best chance was to leave right away.

Every morning at Dinosaur Park, interpreters check the weather just to prevent situations like this, even watching the weather radar on our computers. Rain clouds appear on the screens as amoeba-like blobs making their way over a map of southwest Alberta. A growing blob on a collision course with the park often means programs are cancelled until the rain passes and the ground has time to dry out.

On that particular morning, there had been no blobs in sight and no rain in the forecast, so I had led a very casual, unhurried tour. We made stops along the meandering road until the bus eventually climbed the steep drive to the cliff face with the hadrosaur shelter.

Now, the black clouds made it look like a completely different day.

Calmly, I informed the two women that we would be wrapping up the tour a bit early and that they should head for our small tour bus.

A cloud of sand engulfed us as we stepped outside, stinging our bare arms and faces, finding its way down our shirts, and falling into little piles on the steps of the bus as we entered. I slammed the bus doors behind us, shutting out the sand and wind.

Flipping on the two-way radio, I heard only static. I switched to a second channel to report my situation but found only squawks and broken bits of sentences coming through.

Tornado? A voice on the radio had definitely said the word "tornado."

The wind had become strong enough to rattle the bus, so I decided to get off of the high, exposed hillside and descend to the canyon below. I drove down the steep hill, and just as I reached the bottom where the road levelled out, the rain started. It was a biblical rain that quickly reduced the visibility ahead to zero, forcing me to stop.

"Is this normal?" asked one of the women as the rain pounded the bus.

I turned around, smiled, and calmly tried to make it sound like this was all very expected. Storms were common in summer, I assured them, and they usually passed within a matter of minutes. We were so fortunate to get a front row seat at this show of nature's power. Did they get storms like this where they live in New Jersey?

That's when the hail began. The hammering on the roof of the bus was deafening and I really did think it might shatter the windscreen. I could see some of the road ahead, so I slowly drove forward, watching carefully for places that the road might have washed out as it sometimes did in heavy rains.

The back end of the bus shifted sideways, the tires spun out, and we splashed through a creek that had not been there when we drove in. Many minutes later, just as we reached the park's campground, blue skies appeared overhead as the storm either moved on or wore itself out. We drove past flattened tents and around huge cottonwood fallen across the road. I would learn later that the very first blast of wind had knocked down an antenna, cutting our radio communications. Environment Canada had issued a tornado warning but no tornado had formed. Just the best (and worst) storm that I've yet experienced.

I turned to thank my visitors for coming on the tour and asked if they would like me to drop them off at their car in the parking lot. Their eyes were wide.

"No," one replied. "Please take us to the bathroom!"

"Yes," agreed the other. "To the bathroom!"

Editors' Tips

When faced with a sudden change in the weather during a program:

- Prepare beforehand and check the weather forecast before setting out.

- If you are in an area that is prone to sudden weather changes, pack extra supplies to offer your participants. Having extra rain ponchos, a tube of sunscreen, or a dry pair of socks on hand may just save your program and your reputation.

- Communication is key for safety. Explore using various devices, such as cell phones, radios, and satellite phones.

Dark Times
Night Programs

Night programs are fascinating, provocative, and popular. But they are also challenging and have led many an interpreter to some of their 'darkest' moments.

Grave Tales Sprinklers

Disaster Zone: Town of Fort Langley, British Columbia

Amandeep (Amn) Johal, Interpretation Coordinator
Fort Langley National Historic Site, British Columbia

Grave Tales has been a popular program delivered by Fort Langley National Historic Site for nearly a decade. Offered in the evenings during the month of October, this time of year is often regarded as the time when the veil between our world and the next is the thinnest.

Heritage Interpreters lead groups of people by the light of a lantern as they walk through the cemeteries of the town, and share true stories of those who lived before us, as well as local ghost stories. The tour ends inside the actual fort, where more ghost stories are shared in the buildings and around a bonfire.

On one such walk (the last tour of the evening, actually), I was leading my group of 25 people into what we call "The Pioneer Cemetery." We were already one hour into the tour, and I knew that I had all of their attention. When the tour first began, everyone was laughing and chatty, but after my stories of First Nations burial boxes, a murderous man with a hatchet, and a sailor's hand amputation while he was awake, all I could hear was the light wind through the trees.

Once inside the cemetery - the second one we had visited - I explained that although there were not many grave markers around us, we were in fact standing above two-dozen people buried by the Hudson's Bay Company in the 1800s. We knew who was buried here, as well as how the bodies were laid out. We just did not know which body belonged to which person.

That's when we heard a sound. It was a gurgling, hissing, almost a burp. It sounded similar to what a zombie would sound like on a TV show. I was not sure what was going on, but when I looked at my audience, more than half of them had watery eyes. That's when they began to scream, grab one another and run every which way. A second later, the sprinklers in the lawn activated. The sound we heard was merely the water rushing through the pipes.

As it turned out, the sprinklers were set on a timer. The church next door assumed they had been turned off by the caretaker earlier in the fall, and therefore didn't warn us when we made arrangements to go through their cemetery in the middle of the night.

After we recovered from thinking our lives were going to be over, we found ourselves soaked and laughing.

Editors' Tips

When faced with leading tours in an unfamiliar area:

- Visit the site beforehand at the time you expect to be leading the program. A practice run may prevent a soaked audience.

- Contact landowners and neighbours during planning to make sure there are no surprises.

- Speak with other interpreters or staff that are familiar with the area. You can gain a lot of valuable information from others.

The Night Hike

Disaster Zone: Aundeck Omni Kaning First Nation, Ontario

Peter JF Stobie, CHI, Education Director
Kalamazoo Nature Centre, Kalamazoo, Michigan

Several years ago, I was invited to the Aundeck Omni Kaning First Nation on the North Shore of Manitoulin Island in Ontario. Laura, a teacher and friend of mine from Michigan, has friends on the reserve and arranged for me to deliver some programs to the community.

One of the programs I led was a night hike. I consulted Laura about my planned activities to make sure everything was respectful of Anishinabek culture. Laura warned me that the sudden presence of an owl is a death omen, so I should ask for permission if I wanted to do owl calling. Our audience consisted of approximately five women and seven children. When I asked them if calling owls would be okay, the ladies smiled and politely nodded.

On the hike, I led many activities to interpret the night and help our group become accustomed to the dark. We let our eyes adjust and did some classic activities: disappearing heads, the pirate's patch, frog calling, and finally the owl calls... to no avail. We were close to the lakeshore, yet still in the woods. The setting was perfect.

Finally, it was time for me to facilitate the solo hike. This is where each person walks a set part of the trail on their own. I explained to the group the importance of complete silence and asked them to respect everyone's experience. I told them that I would leave them to go a little further up the trail. Then, I would wait as, one by one, they would walk to me in the dark. Since we had younger ones, I allowed them to walk with a sibling or parent if necessary.

I left and once I was far enough away and out of sight, I stopped and waited. After a couple of minutes, the first participant silently walked towards me and waited with me. We then saw two children come towards us, quietly giggling until they, too, joined us. Suddenly,

I heard many voices and the fast scuffling of feet. The rest of our group, including Laura, rapidly approached us and were obviously spooked. I realized that the solo walk was definitely over, but I wasn't sure why. They briefly explained that they had seen a "white presence" and that they were not sticking around to see it closer. We slowly continued back on the trail and I calmed down the group by focusing their attention on the final activity: Spark in the Dark. We stood in a circle and I passed out Wintergreen Lifesavers. We crushed the candy with our teeth, and watched the sparks ignite in our mouths. We returned to the community center and no one mentioned the events during the solo walk.

Since then, Laura has returned to the reserve several times. She told me that the participants talk highly of their experience on the night hike to this day. However, we both agree that we learned from that experience. Perhaps, doing the owl calls heightened their nerves. And, although they smiled and nodded, they may not have actually wanted me to do it. They simply might not have wanted to appear rude. If the opportunity comes up again, Laura and I would skip the owl calls to be more respectful. And, in terms of the presence that evening, people clearly felt something and were definitely spooked, so I will keep an open mind and respect their culture and beliefs.

Editors' Tips

When faced with interpreting to people from different cultures:

- Be respectful and understanding of different points of view, and be open to learning from your group.

- If someone from the community has arranged the program, they may be willing to help facilitate it. Ask them to introduce you, and be sure to accept their efforts to host you.

- Remember that there is variety within every cultural group. Don't assume that everyone is the same just because they belong to a group. Generalizations and assumptions cause many misunderstandings.

Whooooo Calls Back?

Disaster Zone: Charleston Lake Provincial Park, Ontario

Kenton Otterbein, Natural Heritage Education Specialist
Killbear Provincial Park, Nobel, Ontario

During my first summer as a park naturalist, I was scheduled to lead a night hike. I had previously led lots of night hikes at an outdoor education center, so I thought I knew what I was doing. I planned out the hike with lots of activities for visitors to have a meaningful night-time experience. Forty people showed up for the hike and, like at most night hikes, there was a buzz of nervous excitement in the air.

The hike started and everything was going well. At the last stop, I was building up to the grand finale. I explained that we need absolute silence and that I was going to try and call in a Barred Owl. Everyone was silent as I gave my best "Who cooks for you" call, and then… a cow mooed back in response.

People were crying with laughter and my sense of dignity took a beating. I didn't realize that the trail came so close to a neighbouring farm and I definitely didn't know that a cow would respond to an owl call. I like to think that I somehow managed to wrap up the hike with a meaningful conclusion, but I really have no recollection of how the hike ended, other than that we all had a memorable moment together. For the next few years, the people that were on that hike never failed to mention it to me when they came back to the park.

I did learn a couple of lessons though:

1. Make sure that you test activities in the location and at the time that you are planning to do them. If I had practiced the night before, I might have found out about the cow's response to the owl call and changed the location of the final stop. If it's a hike during the day, you should know where the sun is going to be at different stops so that you can position your group to prevent them from squinting or becoming uncomfortably hot. For night hikes, obviously, the phase of the moon

will affect how dark the night will be.

2. Mother Nature can be rather unpredictable and you have to be able to adapt. Seize the teachable moment when it happens. The more research you do and experiences that you have outside will prepare you for some of those surprises. As another example of a rookie mistake, I was leading a guided hike and I heard the call of a Red-shouldered Hawk approaching. I excitedly told everyone about this rare hawk that was coming our way, and then a Blue Jay burst into view and gave the call of the hawk. That's when I learned that Blue Jays could mimic Red-shouldered Hawks. Of course, you can't know everything and learning with your audience is memorable for everyone. So, I usually try to give myself some wiggle room when explaining something I'm not sure of (e.g. "It might be x or it might be y" or "I'm not sure but my best guess is …").

3. Don't take yourself too seriously. Sure, you're the naturalist and you're supposed to know it all, but funny things can happen, sometimes at your expense. Roll with it and be gracious. Humour can be a very effective way to make connections with visitors.

Editors' Tips

When faced with planning a night walk:

- Make sure you are comfortable being alone at night. Your audience will look to you for support.

- Be sure to conduct multiple practice runs during the time of the program. You will become aware of the "things that go bump in the night" and can set your audience's expectations accordingly.

- Aww, who are we kidding? We all get a little scared of the dark. Bring a friend or coworker along.

Rainforest Night Walk

Disaster Zone: Pacific Rim National Park Reserve, British Columbia

Sherry Kirkvold, Freelance Interpreter/Naturalist

From time immemorial, we humans have been fascinated with darkness. As we come face to face with the unknown, our imaginations run wild. At least, that is what happened to me on the Rainforest Trail in Pacific Rim National Park back in the mid 1980s.

I had created night programs in other parks. One of my most successful programs, Creatures of the Dark, took place my very first night at Alice Lake Provincial Park. As I spoke about bats in the outdoor amphitheatre, they flew all around us. When I played a recording of a screech owl I had heard calling on previous evenings, it flew into a tree right above us for all to see. The rangers said people were talking about my program all over the campground. With that success in mind, I thought a night walk in the rainforest would make an interesting program. As it turns out, it is a very different experience taking a group on a narrow trail in the dark than to simply have them seated in an amphitheatre.

With the program already advertised, I figured I should preview the walk, so I arrived at the trailhead the night before and peered into the dark forest. With my heart in my mouth I started down the trail. What was that sound? That cold rush of wind? I started to think of "things that go bump in the night." What dangers were hidden in the darkness? Were there bears? Cougars? My thoughts of what would or could happen stopped me dead in my tracks and I could not go in alone.

The night of the program proved it was indeed a topic of great appeal. More than a hundred people showed up. The Rainforest Trail is a narrow boardwalk, and some of it is elevated. There are a few enlarged platforms that usually suffice to hold a group during a walk, but none that could contain a group so large. I had cut red cloth into squares and had elastics to secure them as covers for flashlights—but not that many. The longer waves of red light minimize disturbance, but it was impossible to avoid disturbance with a group that large. Any wildlife would be long gone.

With safety in numbers, I entered the dark forest, followed by a long line of glowing red lights. You could not call it an interpretive walk, or even a viewing experience. A few people at the front might have experienced some of what I hoped to convey that night, but now I just wanted them all to make it to the end. It took a very long time. As far as I know, everyone came out since there were no missing persons reports the next day.

I had set up one spotting scope and had four pairs of binoculars on hand to look at the night sky after the walk—not enough for the crowd. Most people drifted away, but a smaller group stayed to look at stars, planets, moons, and even a galaxy. One man was taking copious notes, so finally I asked him why. As it turned out, he was Eric Wilson, an author of mysteries for young adults. This event that I thought was a dismal failure turned out to be perfect for some of the descriptions that later appeared in his book Spirit in the Rainforest.

Those first, tentative steps into the dark forest later became a meaningful and fun program, once we found a way to cope with the numbers. We turned the night walk into a special event and moved it to a more suitable location, where it continued to draw large crowds. Visitors joined one of three groups that rotated between different naturalists. I continued to lead the forest walk, while another naturalist led a beach walk (always special when bioluminescence was present on the sand), and a third tended a campfire for hot chocolate, stories, and stars.

The night program taught me that visitors can have a great experience stepping out of their comfort zone when provided with the proper framework. I now work in the ecotourism industry. The activities are different - I spend a lot of time taking people to watch bears - but the lessons I learned that night long ago help me ensure that these experiences are both exciting and safe.

Editors' Tips

When faced with a larger than expected audience:

- Be honest and apologetic about the problem. Generally, people are understanding and patient if they realize what the situation is.

- Do what you can to accommodate the larger audience - call in a co-worker, ask people to group together and share materials, ask half the audience to come back in a hour - but keep safety in mind. It's better to have a disappointed visitor than an injured one.

- Celebrate! You have discovered a topic that people are excited about. Deliver the program again, but do ask people to pre-register.

Oh. No. Not Now.
Technology and Props

There's nothing like a massive projector failure, a prop thief, or the wind stealing your puppet theatre to make an interpreter consider changing careers...

The Rocky Horror Puppet Show

Disaster Zone: Terra Nova National Park, Newfoundland

Gregory Stroud, Visitor Experience Manager
Lake Superior National Marine Conservation Area, Nipigon, Ontario

I sat there, staring at a group of about 50 mortified kids and laughing adults, and wondering what I ever did in my previous life to deserve the punishment I was now receiving. How could things go so wrong, so quickly? There was no escape and nowhere to run. An earthquake, tsunami, or a forest fire would all have been a welcome respite from the embarrassment I was feeling.

I was so excited to start my first job working in Terra Nova National Park. I grew up with the park in my backyard, so when I received the news that I was hired as a summer interpreter (naturalist), I was very excited. I had no idea what an interpreter was, but I was young and full of energy and ready for just about anything. Or, this is what I thought.

One of my job roles was creating and delivering a puppet show with a fellow interpreter. She was the lead hand and worked in the park the previous summer, so I was to follow her lead. We had about a week of training and worked hard at preparing our puppet show. I was not the most animated puppeteer (with only one voice that had a strong Newfoundland accent) but I felt I was ready for our debut.

We loaded up the van with all our gear (or so I thought) and headed to Malady Head Campground located about a 20-minute drive from our main office. It was a beautiful day with the sun shining and warm temperatures, even though the wind was blowing a little stronger than usual.

We arrived at our destination with enough time to set up the puppet theatre. It consisted of a three-piece folding plywood arrangement, similar to the folding science fair boards. It had a hole in the centre section for the puppets to emerge and the rest was painted with a nice forest scene. Our puppet show was an anti-litter program called "The

Smooth, Shiny, Slippery Stone." The plot centered around a shiny stone made of tinfoil and the forest creatures trying to figure out what it was and where it came from.

As we were setting up, we realized (much to our horror) that we could not find the script. We had two beautifully typed-out, laminated copies, but they were left back in the office and it was too late to go back for them. Also, this was a time before cell phones so we couldn't call someone else to bring them to us. We would just have to wing it based on our memories.

Unfortunately, this was not the end of our problems. We were also missing two of the four puppets. Not only would we have to remember the script, but we would also have to tell the story through only half the number of puppets. This was not going well. When we searched for the tinfoil stone that was the main focus of the show, it was missing too. It was now a disaster. We had a quick discussion to formulate a plan to "get through" this program so we could retreat with some dignity. Then, we began our event.

This was improv before improv was invented. We gave a new definition to the term "winging it." Needless to say, it was not the most polished interpretive program. I don't think the kids cared too much because, after all, there were puppets. As long as the two puppets were moving and talking, most kids did not seem to mind.

Did I mention it was a windy day? This is when the event went from a total disaster to our worse nightmare. The next few minutes of my life happened in slow motion. A huge gust of wind caught the puppet theatre and blew it down in front of us, and all we could do was watch. We just sat there in front of the audience, each with one puppet in the air and 50 sets of eyes staring at us - the kids horrified and the adults all laughing. That is when I wished for a natural disaster so we could escape without any scars, but it was too late. There was nothing to do except take the puppets off, pick the theatre up, go back around, and continue the show. We tried to incorporate the wind into the program to make light of the situation since we were improvising anyway, but really, all I wanted to do was finish the program and run for the hills.

So, here are the two main things I learned from my first ever puppet show:

1. Physically touch everything that you need for your program. Don't just think or assume everything is packed. I now make a rule of touching every puppet, every script, and every prop before I go to a program.

2. Ensure that you have planned for weather conditions. If it is windy, use tent pegs to pin down your theatre. If it is raining, have a backup plan to stay dry. If it is sunny and hot, think of ways to stay in the shade. If the bugs are bad, have bug repellent.

Editors' Tips

When faced with a massive prop failure:

- Create a checklist of props required for a program, and check it EVERY time you deliver a program.

- Go through your prop containers before leaving for a program to ensure you aren't missing anything - or taking the wrong container!

- If you notice during a program that there is an issue with a prop (it is falling apart or your puppet theatre has trouble standing upright), fix it BEFORE you put it away, or you may forget to fix it.

- If the disaster is too big to divert, acknowledge it with humility and humour. Your audience will likely feel your pain and forgive you.

Fur Seal Porn

Disaster Zone: Whiteshell Provincial Park, Manitoba

Heather Graham-Nakaska
Hague, Saskatchewan

During the summer of 1995, I was a park interpreter at a provincial park in Manitoba. We had just added a video projector to our amphitheatre equipment, so we added Thursday Night Movies to our weekly events. Most weeks, the head interpreter would run the movie, talk up our weekend events, and Movie Night became the easiest event ever. One week in July, the head interpreter had to be away, so I was in charge. No problem! Our conservation officer had loaned us a collection of nature movies, including some episodes of Marty Stouffer's Wild America. So, all I had to do, I thought, was pop one in the VCR and press play.

Thursday night rolled around – warm, and clear, with a light breeze to keep the mosquitoes at bay. Families streamed in from the campgrounds, and other park staff came from the bunkhouses on their way to wing night at the bar. Movie Night began with sweeping panoramas, inspiring music, an introduction from Marty Stouffer, and the episode title on the amphitheatre screen: "Living with Wildlife."

Most of the episode is still a blur to me. I remember scenes of some questionable and outdated wildlife practices, a bear tearing up a campsite, and one scene that still appears in my nightmares. I don't remember the set-up, but suddenly we were treated to the mating rituals of the fur seal. Did you know that fur seals mate in a huge writhing heap of slippery flesh, topped off by the master breeder who mates with the entire harem? Neither did I, but everyone in attendance became instantly and graphically well-informed. Next scene, please, next scene, please!

Marine mammal porn is one way to make an interpretive impression. I was "very busy" in the projection booth instead of chatting with visitors as they filed out of the amphitheatre that evening and I "forgot" to promote the weekend's events. With any luck, I wouldn't see these park visitors again. The other staff members were a different story. One girl on the maintenance team lived across the hall from me in the bunkhouse, and she was helpful enough to ask me every day, "How's the harem master?" and "What's the sex-ed movie this week?"

The moral of the story is this: NEVER show a movie that you have not personally previewed. It doesn't matter if your boss gave it to you, or you saw it once in junior high, or you've seen other episodes of the same series; you need to preview it for the context and the audience at hand. The fur seal mating was awful and awkward, but it was only one of many parts of that movie that were irrelevant to the park we were in.

Would 20-year-old me have noticed that the show had very little that related to Manitoba's parks if I'd previewed it? I'd like to think so. But, I know for certain that I would have noticed the master breeder and his mates. If I had, I would have chosen a different movie, or skipped the whole thing and joined the gang for wings.

Editors' Tips

When faced with choosing videos for movie night:

- Always preview the film to make sure it is appropriate for your audience.

- Err on the side of caution and research potentially controversial films. There are websites available that identify family friendly media.

- Don't be tempted to let a movie night just be 'filler' in your program schedule. Choose films that are relevant to your site, and introduce them in a way that helps your audience understand the connection.

Mouse in the Machine

Disaster Zone: Murphy's Point Provincial Park, Ontario

Kathy McPherson

In 1984, I was a seasonal interpreter at Murphy's Point Provincial Park, south of Ottawa, Ontario. The park had a relatively new amphitheatre and I was training my two summer students how to use it. The morning was supposed to be hands-on training about using the amphitheatre equipment, with a healthy dose of everything else they needed to know about running a program there.

I, the consummate professional, began by talking about the importance of arriving early to set up and greet visitors as they arrive. Then, I revealed the trick to lifting the "garage door" that covered the projection screen. Next, it was time to show the students how to operate the 16mm projector. While giving them a running commentary on how to do everything, I showed the students how to place the projector for maximum projection, and demonstrated how to trim the edge of the film and insert it into the appropriate slot. I turned the projector on.

There was a sudden grinding sound, immediately followed by a mouse popping out of the projector and scurrying away, followed by my fleeing staff. Closer examination revealed another mouse, completely killed by turning on the machine, now crushed into the projector.

The projector was out of commission for the summer. The repair store had to leave it outside for a month because of the dead mouse smell. And, even when it was fixed, the smell of crushed mouse never went away.

The moral of the story:

Anticipate potential damage to equipment, and store accordingly. We had a mouse problem at the park, but I foolishly thought that locking the projector in the amphitheatre was enough. I never expected the mice to build a nest in the guts of the machine!

Always have a back-up plan. The park couldn't afford a second projector, but I did find one to borrow.

Work with a sense of humour. After the initial shock, and feeling bad for killing the mouse, we took it in stride and made back-up plans for everything. And, we laughed about it!

Editors' Tips

When faced with preparing for a new interpretive season:

- Check all your equipment before the year's programing starts.

- At the end of the season, make sure your equipment is cleaned and properly stored out of reach of any unwanted inhabitants or users.

- Don't accept 16mm projectors for your site. Demand better. This is the 21st century, for goodness sake!

Missing Deer Antler

Disaster Zone: Balsam Lake Provincial Park, Ontario

Sheila Wiebe, Education Specialist
Bronte Creek Provincial Park, Burlington, Ontario

I was working in a provincial park - let's call it Alsambay Akelay. I was freshly graduated from university, and employed for the summer as the Interpretive Program Leader. It was my first time leading interpretive programs. I was keen to make a good impression and also a little over confident, like many new graduates tend to be.

I had just returned from our regional interpreter training workshop, where I had attended a guided walk about deer led by a seasoned interpreter. I was awestruck and immediately began thinking how I could do a similar program in my park. I "borrowed" some of the hike content, prop ideas, and presentation concepts, adapting them slightly to fit me and my park.

The big difference with this demonstration hike and others I had seen before was that most of the props, including bulky antlers and a heavy garbage bag of deer browse, were all placed along the trail at pre-determined locations where the interpreter wanted to stop. The props were marked with tags that read, "Park Program Equipment. Please leave here." I thought this was a stroke of genius.

When the hike began, I had my marked props hidden along the path and 25-30 campers assembled, eager to learn about white-tailed deer in Alsambay Akelay Provincial Park. The welcome and introduction went fine. I had their interests piqued! Kids were asking questions and telling stories, and parents were tagging along happily. I thought, "This is the greatest job ever!"

Then, I came to the spot where my antler was supposed to be, and discovered that it was gone. Vanished. Now what was I going to do?

I turned to my audience and explained the situation. I carried on with the program as best I could, trying to calm my anger and relay the information without my props. "Imagine, if you will, a solid, bone-like antler…" Finally, it was time to move onto the next stop, where I had stashed a jaw bone.

It was also gone. I felt like crying, "WHY me?" I instantaneously went through the five stages of grief. Denial: This can't be happening! Anger: How dare they! Bargaining: Please, let the other props be there! Depression: This is the worst job ever. And lastly, Acceptance: So what if the props are gone, I can do this!

I managed to finish the hike, relaying the content without the all-important physical artifacts. Each and every one of the props, including deer antlers, jaw bones, and full skulls that had taken me years to find and clean, had been taken from their hiding places, and none were ever recovered. They were also never replaced.

Looking back, I realize the problem was that I had created a cookie-cutter program that relied on the props. Now, I try to be ready for interpretive moments with games, activities, and scenarios to support my topic or theme at my disposal, but I don't rely on props to MAKE my program anymore.

Happily, this experience did not deter me from continuing in the field of interpretation. Twenty-five years later, I can safely say that I have not made this same mistake again, although I have made others and I continue to learn from them.

Editors' Tips

When faced with missing props:

- Carry around some extra props in your backpack, just in case.

- Instead of laying them out with a tag saying "do not remove," try hiding them where they can't be seen, such as behind a bush or rock. Just remember where you hid them.

- Always have extra activities and stories you can use at a moment's notice.

Gunning for Disaster

Disaster Zone: Frank Slide Interpretive Centre, Alberta

Monica Field, Area Manager
Frank Slide Interpretive Centre, Crowsnest Pass, Alberta

I've worked as an interpreter for more than 30 years. Most of this time has been spent at the Frank Slide Interpretive Centre in Alberta's Crowsnest Pass. It's a landscape that is home to tragedy. Alberta's three worst disasters have taken place within sight of my office. Death lies at my doorstep.

Part of the allure in conveying disaster stories involves immersing the audience in a defining moment in time. I try to transport people to a turning point from which there is no escape. I attempt to take the audience there and leave them on the precipice while exposing them to each passing second.

How do I ferry visitors to yesterday's cliff faces? My favorite tools are music, powerful images and drama. Perhaps my most emotional creation is a theatre performance I designed to capture the heartbreaking story of Canada's worst mine disaster, the 1914 Hillcrest Mine explosion.

Back in the day of tape recorders and slide projectors, I delivered my Hillcrest program using historical images of the town, the people, the day of the disaster and the aftermath. I played a song I'd written, a real tear-jerker. And, dressed in historical costume, I concluded the program by assuming the role of a woman named Julia who, eight years old at the time of the disaster, lost her father that fateful day. This factual accounting of events exposes the audience to the poignant outer edge of sorrow and unfathomable loss.

The program, if done to perfection, leaves audiences in shocked and mournful silence. Tears stream down the faces of many viewers, and sobs of grief are common.

The program is a one-woman show, and difficult to deliver. It was particularly problematic back in the '80s when I had to use a remote control to advance the slide projector, positioned behind the audience, while dimming the theatre lights. Then, in complete darkness, I had to push a tape recorder button to play my previously recorded song, Hear That Whistle Blow, which was on a tape along with other songs I'd written and performed.

I'd play the song while controlling the slide projector to display a collage of historic images, then turn off the projector and tape recorder while performing a dramatic vignette in which I became a lady in England who was reading a letter from her brother, a reverend forced to deliver graveside eulogies for the deceased miners.

I had to increase the in-theatre lighting for the vignette, then turn the lights off to set up—quickly—for the final scene, my portrayal of Julia, the program's coup de grace.

The audience was seated, and the lights were off. I crept to the front of the theatre, the slide projector's remote control in my hand, and reached for the tape recorder's play button. There, at a critical crossroads, I inadvertently hit rewind. This destroyed my carefully pre-set positioning of the tape. Frantically, I punched fast-forward and held it down long enough to guess that I might have re-established the appropriate setting.

I hadn't. As the first stark image of the Hillcrest Mine Disaster appeared on the screen, it was accompanied by upbeat mandolin and guitar music from the Hay Fever Kid. It's a funny song I wrote to tell the tale of an Old West gunfighter who, great shot that he was, suffered from chronic hay fever: "Life isn't easy for a guy who gets sneezy..."

Cheerful music and a silly song turned my program upside down. I ended up cutting out the music because I didn't dare try to guess again where I was on the tape. Instead, I decided to narrate the story of the disaster as the slides came up on the screen. But, I was rattled and I'm sure I didn't do the sad story justice. I skipped the vignette and didn't even try Julia's story – what was the point? That was one time I didn't see people crying when they left the theatre.

I cite this example when training new interpreters. It illustrates the value of sound preparation, making sure you don't set yourself up for failure. But above all, it suggests that you can walk the edge, fail spectacularly and, if you're lucky, survive and go on to steal the next show. I also tell new interpreters to remember that most of the stories they're telling are so amazing they require nothing more than simple skills and techniques.

In the days following the described incident, I carried a small flashlight and looked very carefully to ensure that, when I reached for the tape recorder in a dark theatre, I hit play, and that the music was pre-set to complement the image-illustrated story. Never again would the Hay Fever Kid be allowed to set foot in the Hillcrest Mine.

Editors' Tips

When faced with a technological glitch:

- Remember that nobody else knows what your program is supposed to look like. If it seems like the problem can't be fixed easily or quickly, just go ahead without the technology. Your audience may not even notice the difference.

- If you aren't sure how to fix the problem, check your audience for experts. There may be a genius in the second row who can fix everything in 10 seconds. When she fixes it, lead the audience in a round of applause.

- If a technology failure means your program cannot go ahead, then reconsider your program plan. Always have a backup plan in place.

Headless Hobby Horse

Disaster Zone: Kananaskis Country, Alberta

Scott Mair

A talented colleague and I were preparing for our first ever session at an interpretation conference. We were going to share bits and pieces of programs to demonstrate the use of original music and theatre in Kananaskis Country, Alberta. Elvis the Elk was going to bugle, a puppet named Ovis was going to show how to bring puppets to life, and we were going to do a little calypso number I'd written on the North-West Mounted Police. You may think the North-West Mounted Police and calypso music don't seem to go together, but when our two intrepid Mounties ride in on hobby horses in this tongue-in-cheek look at foothills history, it sets a fun, engaging, and slightly irreverent tone that matches the rest of the program.

During each succeeding chorus, the hobby horses get used in increasingly ridiculous ways. Rehearsing the scene for our presentation, we got a little more carried away than usual and were soon swinging our hobby horses in a style more suited to baton twirlers. Suddenly, as we spun the horses around majorette style at the end of the song, one of the heads flew off and went flying across the room. The rehearsal ground to a halt as we rolled on the floor laughing.

Then, we had a brainstorm. What if the head 'accidentally' flew off during the performance? Well, it turns out that it has the same effect on the audience as it did on us. The audience was in stitches!

My favourite response was from a friend's wife. She had been dragged to a few sessions where the Mounties were showcased. After the third time, she turned to my friend and whispered, "You know, I think that's supposed to happen!"

I learned two things from our disaster. Be open to accidents - sometimes they're just what your program needs. And, rehearsal is a great place for your disasters to happen.

Editors' Tips

When planning a disaster on purpose:

- Consider how often your audience will see the same performance. If you are likely to have repeat visitors, mix it up. Do it during some performances, and not at others.

- Always perform as if it is the first time. It might not be as funny if it doesn't feel spontaneous.

- Take advantage of unexpected mistakes, as genius lurks in serendipity.

Hello? Anybody There?

Audiences and Kids

The best thing about an interpretive program is the reaction of the audience. Sometimes, it's also the worst thing.

Halfway There

Disaster Zone: somewhere in California

Marisol Asselta Castro

It was a rousing success, except for the part where we utterly failed.

There's a town in California with a name you'll find on strawberry packages in grocery stores throughout the United States. It's a town of Spanish-speaking farmworkers who are surrounded by primarily Caucasian, English-speaking, upper class residents. It's the only town in the area that doesn't have a free and easily accessed public beach. It's the only town that can get up to 90% unemployment during a bad strawberry year. It's the only town where most of the residents can't afford to buy a home, due to the prices driven up by San Francisco commuters willing to drive over an hour for cheaper housing. Agricultural fields blanket the area, both organic and ones covered with red-striped plastic sheets indicating methyl bromide injections. Children serve as translators for their parents, and parents work in the fields in hopes that their children won't have to work there. In a municipal park, seemingly dropped in the middle of this town, you'll find our little nature center.

Our center is based on wetlands preservation, as almost everything here was built on a wetland. Funding comes from a mandatory fee in residents' water bills and can only be spent to promote water conservation. For the first time ever as an interpreter, I had almost no budget restrictions. Whatever we thought would be helpful, we got. It was magical, and a little dangerous. Our old displays were replaced with brand new exhibits in English, Spanish, and the local Ohlone language. We had a children's play corner, a 3-D touchable map of the watershed, a full-sized recreation of a kitchen and yard to show how daily actions affect the bay, shiny brochures, and timeline-based wall murals from ancient times to current day. It was beautiful. What didn't we have? Visitors. Specifically, the Latino visitors that filled the park to picnic with their families, or walked through on their way to and from work.

In spite of the bilingual "Free Nature Center" signs, they were unsure if this was a place where they belonged. Word of mouth was our slow but sure way to bring in the Latino community, and children were our best liaisons. They'd shyly poke their heads in, asking if they were allowed to enter. Older siblings would follow, then mothers, fathers, cousins, grandparents, and neighbours. The menfolk would wander around at first, smiling distractedly until their interest was sparked with a free faucet aerator or a container for used motor oil. Then, the stories and questions would come.

It was never a fast process, though, and my supervisors at City Hall were hoping to speed things up. After completely renovating the center, we started brainstorming ideas. How could we get people in the door to discover what their water bills have funded? A bilingual live animal program? Excellent! Which animals? How about a slightly scary one that can attract the attention of both children and adults, one that lives in both the US and Latin America…bats, perhaps? Perfect! We contacted the interpreters from a bat education and habitat preservation group, and invited them to come out. Over the next month we jumped into the familiar work of preparation and advertising: writing press releases for local newspapers, creating community calendar events postings, and doing media interviews. The word was getting out. We abandoned the slow pacing of word of mouth and the uncertainty of relying on children translating to their parents.

In one sense, we were successful in the outcome. Eighty people - mostly parents with young children - packed the little nature center, excited and impatient to see the bats hidden in their covered cages. I had my volunteers standing by, and was prepared to translate for the Spanish-speaking visitors. There was only one small problem. Absolutely nobody in the room spoke Spanish. The eighty people packing our center were all caucasian, English-speaking residents of the wealthier surrounding towns. You know, the people that regularly get all the newspapers that published our press releases, articles, and community calendars.

It's a funny thing when you're trying to cut corners. The intentions were good: do a big event to draw people in. Reach out to the community. Announce that your exhibits and programs are bilingual and free for everyone. The only problem was that we were unwilling to meet people where they actually were. Most Spanish-speaking folks won't read an ad, even in Spanish, in an English-language newspaper. Most people in a community that depends on word of mouth aren't going to come to an event that nobody they know has even heard of. In a town where a significant number of people are undocumented immigrant farmworkers, no live bat program is worth risking showing up where you might not be wanted. We wanted faster results, and maybe also wanted to stay a bit in the comfort zone of familiar tactics. There's nothing quite as impressively ineffective as announcing that you want to do something different and immediately following it up by doing the exact same thing you were doing before.

Not all was lost, though. Several of those children that would peek in the door became my regular volunteers. I scrambled them like fighter jets to patrol the park and tell picnicking families that, "¡Un evento gratis con murciélagos vivos está ocurriendo en el Centro de Naturaleza ahora!" In the end, we had about a dozen people come in that were able to translate for each other, and word of mouth saved the day. Months afterwards, we had visitors stopping in to ask about a live animal event they heard was happening.

Lesson learned. In the rush for community engagement, don't outrun your community.

Editors' Tips

When faced with promoting a program to a new audience.

- Enlist a champion from that specific target market (community leader, etc.) to help promote it from within.

- Consider the audience's barriers (price, transportation, etc.). Why aren't they already attending? Actively work to remove those barriers. You may need to completely revamp your approach.

- Don't make assumptions about your audience. Ask questions instead to better understand them.

Unicorns are Real

Disaster Zone: Parks Canada Discovery Centre, Ontario

Paul Bruneau
Parks Canada, Gatineau, Quebec

It was early in my interpretive career. A large group was visiting our site, and I was taking a smaller group through our exhibits on a tour. I can't identify the group precisely; that's part of the problem. Perhaps they were Mormon or Amish or Hutterites; I'm not sure. The women were dressed in long dresses, and some of them wore white caps or hats on their head. They arrived on a large bus, and I wasn't sure if the group was part of the same family, or simply a group travelling together.

During one of the usual stops in our gallery, I took out a narwhal tusk that was often used as an interpretive prop. It was quite popular and many visitors found it to be quite fascinating. It was pretty cool! Not knowing my audience particularly well (as evidenced in my first paragraph), I began to interpret the tusk, and mentioned that many believe the narwhal tusk is where the idea of the mythological creature, the unicorn, came from. Oops….

Shortly thereafter, I was interrupted mid-speech by the father figure (or guide; again, I'm not sure).

"Excuse me!?" he said. "Mythological? I'll have you know that the unicorn is referenced in the Bible, and is not a myth."

I did my best to salvage the moment and turn an awkward situation into something more positive. I believe I succeeded at this. I shook it off, as I had no way of knowing the particulars of his religion, or what might be in the Bible associated with his particular faith. I did, however, exercise more caution when sharing the narwhal / unicorn story in the future.

As it turns out, some of our visitors do believe that unicorns are real.

Editors' Tips

When faced with an audience member who disagrees with you:

- Acknowledge the alternative viewpoint and carry on. You don't have to debate an issue in front of the whole audience.

- If appropriate, you can discuss the issue with the individual after your program.

- Remember that your job as an interpreter isn't to tell others how they should think. Your job is to provide thoughtful information and experiences so that they can make up their own minds.

Missing Teacher

Disaster Zone: John Janzen Nature Centre, Edmonton, Alberta

Margot Hervieux, Operations Manager
Northwest Region Alberta Parks, Alberta

When I delivered elementary school programs at an urban nature centre, I had many different experiences with the teachers who brought their classes for field trips.

Some teachers didn't step up to help manage their students. Others distracted the entire group by chatting with parents at the back. Equally challenging, some teachers answered questions that were meant for the students. Worse still, some even shared misleading or distracting information at inappropriate times.

Perhaps the oddest, however, was the time when an older teacher simply disappeared once I began the program with her class. For the entire two hour walk, I would glimpse her off in the woods. She was always nearby but never part of the group. When the program was over, she finally rejoined us to say goodbye and load her students on the bus. I don't recall that the class was a particular challenge and will never know why she chose to "take a break" from the students.

In talking to other interpreters, I've realized that scenarios like this are not uncommon.

There is a lot of planning that goes into a school program. Interpreters often focus all their energy on the activities and their own group management skills, such as setting boundaries and giving clear directions. I learned from the Disappearing Teacher that the role of teachers (and parent volunteers) also has to be carefully considered when planning these types of programs.

We always did call teachers in advance for these programs to discuss details, but never thought to specifically say that the teacher needed to stay with the class…

Editors' Tips

When faced with unsupportive adult helpers during school programs:

- Many teachers may hold back on disciplining their class during a field trip because they don't want to undermine you as the group leader. If you want them to take a more active role, just ask for help.

- If teachers are chatting in the background or otherwise distracting the class, include them when you explain rules. "And this applies to everyone, including the adults.... Mr. Smith?"

- Create a handout outlining your expectations for adult helpers. Share it with teachers when they book programs, and ask them to go over it with any adults accompanying the group.

- Rethink how many adult helpers you actually need. If there are fewer adults accompanying the group, they will each have more to do, and be less likely to distract the kids.

The Lost Kid

Disaster Zone: Calgary, Alberta

Don Enright, Freelance Interpretive Planner
Vancouver, British Columbia

Over a very long career in interpretation, I've had the usual challenges. There have been drunk audience members, disintegrating props, animals copulating in the middle of a talk… but the darkest moment by far was the day I lost a child.

I was a nature day camp leader in the 1990s. We spent our days hiking around the parks of the region, studying, drawing, and birding. It was fun, rewarding work.

When managing children, of course, one gets in the habit of counting heads. And count I did: getting into the van, out of the van, going to the washroom, and coming from the washroom. I suppose I fell into a kind of magical thinking, that the act of counting heads was somehow a kind of incantation that would protect me from actually losing one.

It was a Friday afternoon and my co-leader had requested some time off. Because we were staying in town, within a city park, my manager had seen fit to grant that time off without replacing my partner, effectively leaving me alone with a dozen kids. In retrospect, that was mistake number one.

We toured a beautiful semi-wild city park, searching under sunny skies for birds and garter snakes and butterflies. We had just stopped in a clearing for a snack break, then gathered our things and moved on. Before leaving, I counted… nine, ten, eleven, twelve. We walked some distance, then stopped to look at a bird, and then I counted again: nine, ten, eleven… eleven… eleven… Hmm. I looked down the trail for a straggler, but saw nobody. Eleven. I had a missing child. In the thirty seconds it had taken to move down the trail, I had lost a boy.

I'm not a person who panics easily. I am usually one of those people who can be relied on to keep a clear head in an emergency. But, I can't recall ever feeling so completely and utterly alone as I did that moment, with eleven children looking up at me. The reality of one of their friends being missing was quickly sinking in. Now what?

I wasn't worried about an abduction. I wasn't worried he'd fallen and hurt himself. The cause of my near-panic was the big, beautiful Bow River right next to us. Spring runoff peaks late in southern Alberta, and the banks of the Bow were swollen to overflowing. It's a dangerous river and has claimed more than a few young lives over the years.

I knew my missing kid was within a stone's throw of those waters, and I needed to find him in a hurry. I had no phone nor radio, nor was there anyone else around—a responsible-looking passer-by, for example— that I could call on for help. I had two choices: grab my eleven kids and high-tail it to the nearest phone, or leave my kids and go looking on my own. I decided, for better or worse, that getting my lost kid away from that riverbank was the highest priority. I would quickly sweep the riverbank, then take the kids and go for help if that turned up nothing.

I moved my eleven kids into a safe clearing, and calmly told them that they were going to pretend to be young deer in a meadow. They needed to stay put no matter what, and stay together, and I would be back in a minute. Did they understand? They all nodded, tears welling up in the eyes of a couple of them. They could see I was scared.

Off I went, running and calling the boy's name, up and down the river's edge. I searched each eddy, each backwater, each crumbling piece of riverbank. Nothing. How far could he have gotten? He had been missing for only a minute and a half. He couldn't be far. He had to be within earshot… unless he was in the river. I called louder. I ran further downstream. Nothing. I felt sick. I ran and zigzagged along the riverbank and screamed his name, until I knew I needed to call for a rescue.

I ran back to my kids in the meadow. They had organized themselves into a stationary search party, God love them, each looking outward, scanning the horizon. They were calling the boy's name in unison every ten or fifteen seconds.

Together, we ran up the trail to the park office, and burst through the doors.

There he was! My missing boy was chewing on a stick of red liquorice and chatting with the receptionist, calm as could be. I asked him if he was ok, and he assured me he was fine. He had stopped to look at a bug, and when he saw that we had moved on, he simply followed the trail toward the office. Wasn't that what he was supposed to do? I hugged him and said yes. Yes, he had done exactly the right thing.

What did I learn from the exercise? Never, ever leave a group of kids with a single leader. Make sure children know what to do if they get separated from the group. Carry a phone or a radio, without fail. Keep your group tight.

And, never let your guard down in the outdoors.

Editors' Tips

When faced with an actual disaster in the middle of a program:

- Take a deep breath and try not to lose your cool. Your audience will be looking to you to decide how to react.

- Familiarize yourself with your site's emergency plans before anything ever happens. And, always bring a form of communication with you to call for help.

- Make sure you do not put other visitors at risk; identify someone as "honorary tour guide" and request the group to stay put while you enact your site's emergency protocols.

- Carry this book with you at all times and refer to the appropriate stories as needed.

Short Shorts

Disaster Zone: Georgian Bay Islands National Park, Ontario

Victoria Evans, Interpretation Coordinator
Georgian Bay Islands National Park, Midland, Ontario

It was a hot and hazy summer afternoon, the kind that brings all the rattlesnakes out of their rocky corners to dart across the campground. When one found its way smack into the middle of a campsite, the park warden was called in to relocate it. I was called in to give an impromptu talk about Massasauga rattlesnakes to the gathering crowd. The audience consisted of whomever happened to be in the area that day, and were drawn in by the uniforms and activity. There were all sorts of people, including a man in his seventies wearing nothing but very, very short jean shorts. Think teenagers on spring break at the Jersey Shore.

As I began sharing some gems of information about pit vipers, he approached closer and closer, inserting "Mm-hmmmms" and delighted "Ahs!" after each little fact. I was glad he was enjoying the talk, but he was getting a little too close for comfort now that he was standing less than a foot away from me. He had actually pushed his way past children to reach the front. "I'm not sure that little guy can see," I said, hoping this would snap him out of his daze so that he would let the kids in front of him. It didn't work.

"Well that's really something, isn't it?" he said, looking at me, instead of the snake.

"Why yes it is! Does anyone know why this snake keeps sticking out its tongue? Anyone…?"

As a little boy raised his hand excitedly to answer my question, Mr. Shorts stepped closer again.

"So what do you do?" he asked me.

"Well, I'm a park interpreter and a trained biologist, so I often give talks on snakes, just like this one! Does anyone know what snakes like to eat?" I asked desperately.

"No," he said, leaning further forward, "what do you do?"

I was speechless. Thankfully, the warden had completed his work and it was time to transfer the snake back into the wild.

"Got to go! This snake has a date with nature!" I explained, as I awkwardly backed away from Mr. Shorts and the rest of the crowd.

He was a remarkably fast walker for a septuagenarian in short-shorts and bare feet. I walked as fast as I could without breaking into a canter, trying to catch up with my colleagues who were thoroughly enjoying the scene. He trailed close behind, inquiring what time my shift ended and trying to sell me on sunsets from his sailboat. I finally lost him by jumping onto the back of a John Deere 'Gator' passing through the campground.

Some interpretive glitches can be avoided with great planning, experience and forethought. Others just saunter right in, wearing only ultra-short jean shorts, and proceed to undo all of your careful planning. Mr. Shorts himself wasn't preventable, but the harassment sideshow probably was. As we often teach our visitors, the worst thing you can do when something charges you is run.

Humour is an excellent weapon against awkwardness, and one I would have used to my advantage if this situation happened again. For instance:

Mr. Shorts: "No, I mean, what do you *do*?"

Cool, calm and collected interpreter: "Well I'm an interpreter. I can turn any awkward situation into a learning experience. For instance – clothing! Snakes don't need it, know why? When their skin gets dirty or worn out they just shed it! Anyhow…"

It's not easy to come up with humourous, effective, and appropriate comebacks on the fly – so, practice! Interpretation always has an element of performance, and some of the most important exercises for performers are improvisation games. Throw situations at each other while you prepare for the season, or on quiet rainy afternoons at work, and you'll develop your skills faster than you would through regular experience and time. And, maybe practice jumping onto the back of moving park vehicles while you're at it.

Editors' Tips

When faced with awkward audience members:

- Consider creating a code word to let coworkers know you need to be rescued: "We need to talk about the _____."

- Use the sidekick trick by enlisting the audience member in assisting you with some menial task. Keeping them occupied with holding a prop will go a long way to reduce awkward moments.

- If you ever feel unsafe due to an audience member, do not hesitate to end the program early, call for help, and/or ask a different audience member to walk back to the office with you.

To Err Is Human
Bad Planning & Human Error

Sometimes there's nothing to blame a disaster on other than plain old human error. Even the most experienced interpreters sometimes forget to turn their microphones off or check the tide tables.

Bathroom Breaks

Disaster Zones: Seward, USA and Townsville, Australia

Sam H. Ham, Professor Emeritus
University of Idaho, USA

Maslow had it right when he anointed biological needs as our number one priority.

By far, my two most embarrassing moments have come during or after restroom breaks. The first happened when I was making a high-profile presentation to an audience of over two hundred interpreters, guides, and tour operators in Kenai Fjords National Park, Alaska. Like any experienced speaker, I made sure to use the restroom just prior to being introduced. Unfortunately, I neglected an essential step.

I began my presentation, and the audience seemed captivated. For ten solid minutes I held the undivided attention of everyone in the audience. They were mesmerized. It was then that I noticed about a dozen participants pointing at my midsection and saying something. All I could hear was collective garble. Finally, unable to tolerate the confusion any longer, I appointed a young man sitting in the back to tell me what was going on. He yelled out, "Sam, your zipper's down!"

There was instantaneous and very loud laughter and I suddenly felt very alone on that stage. To cut the tension, I turned my back to the audience and reached down to zip my pants up, springing into a half jump in order to exaggerate the motion and make a bit of a joke of the whole thing.

When I turned to face my audience again, there was the very best kind of applause - the appreciation an audience shows when they respect your humility, I guess.

There was an even more embarrassing moment during a workshop for about a hundred people in Australia. Suffice it to say that if you use a wireless microphone, you must absolutely remember to mute it before using the toilet!

Editors' Tips

When faced with an embarrassing mistake in the middle of a presentation:

- Try dispelling it with humour.

- When you mess up, fess up - the audience will respond warmly to your humility.

- Remember that this happens to even the most experienced interpreters. Don't beat yourself up for making mistakes.

Potato Carving

Disaster Zone: Sibbald Point Provincial Park, Ontario

Stephanie Yuill, Public Education Coordinator
Department of Environment and Natural Resources, Yellowknife, North-
west Territories

Success can breed confidence; confidence, smugness; and smugness complacency. Complacency should never, ever be in the interpreter's toolkit. These are just some of the lessons I learned during the Great Potato Incident of 2003.

In the spring of that year, a local teacher requested a curriculum-based totem program for her grade three class. We learned what totems are, what they represent and where they are found. We drew animals that are often seen on totems and each child drew their own family totem. The pièce de résistance was the chance to try our hand at carving using a potato and a rock, chosen to replicate the yellow cedar and carving knives that BC First Nations might have used 200 years ago. It was a roaring success.

This is where success bred confidence. It went so well I chose to repeat the program later that season for campers and park visitors.

And this is where confidence bred smugness. I wrote and executed the program so I knew what was needed. I was prepared! The program was advertised in campground bathroom stalls. I arrived 2o minutes early and organized the picnic tables into a circle so I could circulate and encourage the riveted youth.

And this is where smugness bred complacency. In my Rubbermaid container, I had all the necessary props (pictures, maps, actual totems, etc.). It also held a bag of 20 potatoes and a collection of 20 small rocks.

Right on schedule, the children began to stream in: five, ten, twenty, forty. My mind rapidly assessed the blossoming number and figured out how to adapt. Extra rocks were easy. I could collect them off the ground.

Potatoes, however, while admittedly grow in the ground, don't grow on trees. Easy, I thought. I'll cut the potatoes in half so each child had at least something to experiment with.

With no cutting board in my magic Rubbermaid, I took my Swiss Army knife in one hand and a potato in the other and began cutting. Unfortunately, the potatoes weren't the only thing sliced that day. About 8 potatoes in, the knife slipped and plunged into the fleshy centre of my left hand, causing it to start bleeding profusely.

Not wanting the audience to panic, I quickly stuffed my hand into a pocket of my Parks-blue shorts. If I could just get the kids to start carving, it would give me time to do first aid.

I could feel the blood seeping into my shorts as I stood there, clumsily trying to cut a potato in half with one hand. My smile was a grimace but the kids seemed to be having fun and didn't notice anything. Fortunately, a kind and observant parent noticed and came to my aid. She took over the slicing and I was able to bandage my wound and change out of my blood-soaked shorts!

Lessons learned?

Always keep a first aid kit close by.

Always bring too many props, rather than too few.

Most importantly, always ask for help. In my early years as an interpreter, I felt it was my responsibility to be everything: host, comedian, educator, guide, counsellor, nurturer, artist, etc. But people actually like to be involved and help. It makes them feel important and part of the program. So let them! This is a lesson I carry with me today and it has made me a better interpreter, as well as a better person!

Editors' Tips

When faced with a first aid scenario in the middle of a program:

- Make sure that whatever caused the problem (a tripping hazard, a broken display case, a wild animal) is safely dealt with before you provide first aid. You don't want to be the 2nd victim.

- Give your group something to do to keep them occupied (like cutting up the rest of the potatoes) while you help the injured person.

- If you are the one who needs first aid, be professional and try to keep your cool, but don't be too proud to ask for help. Asking for assistance sets an excellent example. And, there might be a nurse or paramedic in your tour group.

Intertidal Stranding

Disaster Zone: Bay of Fundy, New Brunswick

Munju Monique Ravindra

From the very first interpretive program I did over twenty years ago (where an audience member called out "relax, we're on vacation" as I fussed breathlessly with a burnt-out slide projector bulb), to the night walks when I lost the trail, my life-as-an-interpreter is littered with "gulp" moments. Looking back, I like them all; mostly because of what each taught me about how to be a better interpreter, and a better human being in general.

My favourite disaster story is the time when I almost drowned my audience.

I was four seasons into interpretation and only one season into interpreting Fundy National Park on the Bay of Fundy in New Brunswick. The park's specialty was daily 'tide walks' - taking advantage of the world's highest (and lowest) tides to expose visitors to cool animals, such as tube worms and crustaceans. I loved doing the walks, and over the course of my first season at Fundy had become totally engrossed with the flight plan of the Semipalmated sandpiper, the mechanics of a fish weir, and showing people how to lure periwinkles out of their shells by whistling. But, I was always a little jealous of the senior interpreters I emulated. They. Knew. Everything. And, they got to do the special guided walks on the bimonthly spring tide – when the gravitational influence of moon and sun overlap, causing a particularly high (and particularly low) tide. My own programing schedule meant I was never able to attend one of these special walks, but I heard tales of magic and mystery and of creatures resplendent with colour! Groovy as I found them, the mudflat critters were resplendent in shades of, well... brown.

Fast-forward to my second season at Fundy. My supervisor told me that since I was now a 'senior' interpreter, I was to give the spring tide walk. The route was more or less predetermined: I would lead visitors out to a normally underwater reef on a falling tide, look at all the cool stuff, and head back before the tide started to rise again. Having never actually attended this special walk myself, I had no idea what we might find. And, while I was by this time an expert in the sex lives of barnacles, I wasn't sure I would be able to identify anything more exotic than a starfish (which I was trying to remember to call a 'sea star'). So, I loaded up my backpack with every intertidal field guide I could find, some magnifying lenses, and a plastic container to temporarily house our finds. My mother was visiting, so I brought her along to help, because you never know when you'll need your mother, and she was still fascinated by the fact that I knew about things that lived in the sea.

We eagerly set off with a group of about thirty visitors (including five or six young children). After walking across slurpy mud and a few damp barnacle-clad rocks, we arrived at the designated spot - a rocky outcrop with small pools fringed with rockweed. We got right into it: exploring, exclaiming, puzzling, and looking up all this wonderful stuff we encountered in my field guides. There was beauty everywhere: clumps of blue mussels clinging to the edge of the outcrop, saffron-coloured sea stars, prickly sea urchins, endless bizarre worms, unidentifiable clumps of egg-seeming goop, and our big prize – a silver spotted sea anemone.

We were all seriously into it. So into it, in fact, that I didn't lift my head up even once to look around at our surroundings, until my mother materialized at my side, tugging on my shirt and whispering, "Um, I think you should look at the tide." Oops! We were stranded on a rapidly shrinking rock that had gone from outcrop to island during the hours we'd been delightedly ogling sea creatures. Trying to sound as if this was entirely part of the plan, I told the group to gather up the field guides and magnifiers, and to get their backpacks on their backs and ready to go. As they looked goggle-eyed at the rising water, I realized it was time to act. As in theatre. "We'll need to wade!" I said cheerfully, trying to keep the question mark out of my voice. "I think we should carry the kids. The water might be a little deep. Ish."

And, off we set, children precariously balanced on various sets of shoulders, my field-guide-laden backpack held high above my head. We waded slowly through rising tide with water up to our thighs. Everyone stayed very focused; there was no talking, no laughing, and we made it back to dry land without mishap. No one slipped, no one drowned, but everyone got thoroughly soaked. I was horrified. I said goodbye to my now-shivering visitors and staggered back to the office, chagrined, to explain to my supervisor that I had almost drowned an entire group of visitors. Under the circumstances, she was gentle: she gave me a talking-to, warned me to prepare myself for some negative comment cards, and we put the matter to bed.

But, the negative comment cards never came. Instead, we got card after card of positive comments about the visitors' wonderful experience, how their children were inspired to study marine biology, how valuable a place this Bay of Fundy was, and how 'wow!' A week later, the park superintendent received a letter raving about the extraordinary experience that this family had with me (Me! Clueless, disastrously dangerous, un-knowledgeable me!). In particular, they enthused, their children had loved how we had to get off the island at high tide. It was an adventure, it was exciting, and they loved the creatures they had seen.

I learned that a sense of danger (perceived danger, not real danger) can create a very compelling experience, allowing people to feel as if they have achieved something special. This sensation can be created by leading your group across a rushing brook, taking them outside without flashlights in the dark, or challenging them to hike to the top of a certain peak. Essentially, we are providing them an opportunity to transform themselves in the environment we are interpreting. I also learned that as the guides, we are the ones responsible for the situation, and we have to find ways to keep part of our attention on the logistics.

Tips

- Pay attention the logistics of your program (whether in the theatre or on a hike - know where you're going and plan a way to keep track of the time, even if it means setting a vibrate alarm on the phone in your pocket).
- Design your guided hikes with a sense of 'quest' or 'adventure' (but avoid actual danger!)
- If you can, always bring your mother along.

Editors' Tips

When faced with leading a walk in the intertidal zone:

- Always check the tide tables beforehand, and plan accordingly.
- Wear a watch and stick to a schedule. Time and tides wait for no interpreter!

- Allow extra time for walking from place to place with your group, so that you can look at things along the way without feeling rushed.

Ice Cream for Everyone!

Disaster Zone: Sidney Island, British Columbia

Pam Murray, Lead Interpretive Guide
Milner Gardens & Woodland, Qualicum Beach, British Columbia

It was early in my career as an interpreter, and I was working for a contractor in British Columbia Parks, doing many, many school programs, mostly on beaches. One of the most popular programs involved hauling a beach seine net through an eelgrass bed with the class, so that they could see the incredible diversity of creatures that lived there, and gain an appreciation for a habitat that they otherwise could not see.

I got in trouble one day when a particularly cynical group of 5th graders arrived. I introduced the group to eelgrass and showed them the net, then enthusiastically set off down to the beach as I envisioned the mind-blowing formative experience that was about to take place. All of the kids were about to become champions of sensitive intertidal fish habitats!

Everything was going smoothly, until a student asked, "Are we going to catch anything?"

Stupidly, I replied with, "If there's not at least one fish in this net for everyone here, I'll buy you all ice cream!"

Oops.

I quickly led the group in setting the net and organized them into two teams to pull the ropes that bring the net in. When the net arrived on shore, I talked about how to safely pick up the creatures and place them in Ziplock bags of water to bring them to our observation pool. I then led the class to the net to check out the hundreds of fish we had doubtlessly caught.

I began to feel nervous as I realized there was not much moving around in the net. I soon discovered that I had made a huge mistake, and had forgotten to check for tangles in the net before setting it. There was a twist in the middle of the net, resulting in a big space at the bottom, large enough for all of the fish to escape through. Horrified, I began desperately searching for any creatures I could find. I found three or four fish and a number of shore crabs. Meanwhile, ice-cream obsessed children were, I am sure, secretly releasing any fish that we had actually caught.

When the net was empty, which didn't take very long, we gathered at the observation pool.

The group was completely engaged... in counting how many fish we had, as well as reminding me that shore crabs were not fish. It was glaringly obvious that there had NOT been a fish in the net for everyone.

It was the last program of the day, and so I ended up on the same ferry home as the kids. I spent the entire ride awkwardly avoiding questions about what flavour of ice cream I was going to buy them, while doing math in my head to determine just how much this mistake was going to cost me.

When we got off the ferry, the teacher tried to let me off the hook by announcing they would be late getting back to school if we went for ice cream. I, however, felt that if I had totally failed to teach the class anything about eelgrass, I could at least show them an example of coming through on one's promises. I pulled $20 out of my wallet and asked the teacher to use it to buy a bucket of ice cream and some cones, then drove back to the nature house that served as our office, completely embarrassed, where I said nothing of this to anyone.

A few weeks later, a package of thank you letters arrived. My coworkers were all very curious about why this particular class was thanking me for the ice cream.

The ice cream incident taught me to always double-check, and sometimes triple-check, my equipment.

The bigger lesson for me (that was well worth the $20 I paid for it) was the importance of leading interpretive programs with humility. I had let my own expectations, and ego, take over, and ruined the program in the process. I had forgotten that this program I had delivered a hundred times was still a brand new experience for the kids, and didn't need promises of ice-cream to make it exciting. If only I had remained humble, my thank you letters probably would have been covered in drawings of shore crabs rather than ice-cream cones.

Editors' Tips

When faced with setting expectations for your program:

- Keep expectations reasonable. Don't promise the moon - or ice cream, for that matter.

- Know, or ask, what your audience's expectations are at the beginning of the program, so that you can address them.

- The old adage, "Under promise and over deliver" is a great motto. Focus on exceeding expectations instead of struggling to meet them.

Spot Prawn Sex Change

Disaster Zone: Vancouver Aquarium, British Columbia

Nicole Cann, Manager of Interpretive Delivery
Vancouver Aquarium, Vancouver, British Columbia

We used to do this great little gem of a show called "Skin Deep." The premise was simple; it was a beauty pageant for some of the less than adorable animals at the aquarium - creatures like sea cucumbers, nudibranchs, and crabs. We'd bring a few contestants into the theatre in their travel-sized exhibits, project them onto our theatre screen, and then the host would proceed to interview them while another interpreter acted as their voice behind the curtain.

In this particular contest, I was the host. When I was interviewing a British Columbian spot prawn, we discussed the incredible metamorphosis that prawns undergo. They are all born males and then, after a couple of years, they turn into females. After this revelation, I immediately turned to the crowd and said, "WOW! What an amazing transformation! Has anyone here in the crowd undergone something similar?"

Crickets...

I couldn't believe it. I had just asked my entire audience if any of them had ever had a sex change.

I have never heard that sort of silence from a crowd before. As soon as I could manage to speak again, I immediately apologized and tried to move on with the show, but it was obvious that my audience wasn't moving with me. I tried to finish the show as best I could, but I never felt like I truly got my audience, or my confidence, back.

Once the show ended and the audience left, I was mortified. Thankfully, the other interpreter who had been voicing the animal contestants set me straight. He laughed his head off and told me, "Well, you'll never say that again!"

Obviously, I never did.

Sometimes, when you have delivered a program too many times, you might stop thinking about what you are saying. That's when it is easy to make a royal blunder. This incident taught me to never become too comfortable with a program. It may be your hundredth time delivering it, but it is the first time for the audience watching. You have to give it your all and make each and every program your best, and I've endeavoured to remember that ever since.

Editors' Tips

When faced with having just said the wrong thing:

- Fess up. Honesty is the best policy and will be appreciated by the audience.

- Humour is a great way to handle a major flub. Just make sure the humour is in good taste.

- If your mistake was offensive, make sure to sincerely apologize and move on. Don't make excuses - you'll only make it worse.

Of Finches and Men

Disaster Zone: Assiniboine Park Zoo, Manitoba

Cal Martin, Principal
Frog in the Pocket

I must have been told dozens of times. You know, the old maxim repeated at so many interpretive training sessions: Don't be afraid to say, "I don't know". Never – ever – make up information. It seems such like such a simple, easy rule. But, sometimes fate tricks you into learning the hard way.

It was one of my first serious interpretive jobs. A special Australian exhibit was opening at the local zoo, and I was one of a handful of interpreters hired for the summer. We had all kinds of strange new animals arriving for the exhibit: koalas, wallabies, kangaroos, kookaburras, parrots, sharks, black swans, and lorikeets, to name a few. There was so much information to learn, and, as is often the case with interpretive jobs, far too little time before opening.

The strategy we came up with was simple. Each interpreter would thoroughly study two Australian animals. We would then be stationed at these two exhibits the first few days, until we had time to learn about more animals. Slowly, we would build our repertoire until we had each mastered the natural history of the Land Down Under. Easy.

I was assigned my two animals – kangaroos and emus – and I quickly took up my research assignment with the passion and vigour of a young, green, and slightly nerdy interpreter. I learned about different species of kangaroos. I learned about delayed implantation in marsupials. I even learned that emus belong to a group of flightless birds called *ratites* (because we all know that every member of the public wants to know that). After endless hours of study and practice, I was finally ready for the opening day.

Just to make sure that we were all prepared, we polished our presentations for the advanced sneak preview for members and VIPs. I was dying to share all my whiz-bang facts on emus and kangaroos. I even came to the sneak preview an hour early to choose the best vantage point for speaking. Nothing could have prepared me for the rude awakening I was about to receive.

"Unfortunately, neither the emus nor the kangaroos have arrived yet, so they aren't on display," my boss said.

"What?!?" was my feeble response.

"Don't worry. One of the other interpreters has called in sick. We are going to have you cover their animal."

"Which animal?"

"The Australian finches."

So, there I stood in a small building with about fifty tiny free-flying birds, armed only with facts about marsupials and large, flightless birds. I had about twenty minutes to prepare for the arrival of the VIPs. Don't panic, I told myself. Don't panic. I looked around the building for anything that could help me out. Aha! Interpretive panels! I quickly scanned the large colourful panels, looking for identification pictures. Then, I read the text: "These are the names of the finches in this building. Can you tell which is which?"

My heart sank. Okay, I thought. I'm a smart boy. I can figure this out. Sure enough, I was able to slowly determine which finch was which by their somewhat descriptive names. I was identifying the last couple of species when the crowd started to trickle into the building.

My presentation was casual at first. I would chat with a couple of people about the exhibit, avoiding any details, and then move on to the next group. But, invariably, people started to ask questions. I would answer with uncertainty, "You see that bird in the corner? I'm not sure, but that's probably a zebra finch, because of the black on its throat." With every answer, I gained more confidence in my identifications.

Twenty minutes later, I was standing on a crate, delivering big, flamboyant talks to a room packed with people. I was making confident, bold statements and identified all kinds of birds beyond a shadow of a doubt.

That's when it happened. In front of everyone, a thin stranger at the back asked, "Excuse me, but which ones are the zebra finches again?" I had now answered this question dozens of times, and was quite sure about my answer. I replied, "Those birds in the back with the black patches on their throats."

"No, they're not", he said. Everyone was silent. You could have heard a pin drop.

"Why yes, they are. Those are definitely the zebra finches."

"No, actually they're not. I work in the zoo hospital and all the zebra finches are in quarantine."

The crowd stared at me in silence. There was absolutely nothing I could say to fix the situation. Members, donors, board members – they were all in the audience. All of my authority on the subject had vanished in the eyes of the crowd. I just waited for the next group and said, "I'm not sure which finches are which, as I read up on the kangaroos and emus, but let's figure it out together…"

And never again have I made up information. I'm just too scared of that thin stranger in the back of the crowd.

Editors' Tips

When faced with interpreting a subject you don't know much about:

- Don't ever be afraid to say "I don't know."

- If you do ever have to say "I don't know" make sure to research the answer so you will know for the next time.

- If possible, obtain contact information for the person who asked the question. Do your homework and call them with the answer. They will be impressed!

About the Editors

Pamela Murray discovered that interpretation was her calling when her summer job sent her to an Interpretation Canada conference in Manning Provincial Park in 1998. After many years as a front-line interpreter in provincial and national parks in British Columbia and Alberta, she is currently the Lead Interpreter at Milner Gardens & Woodland, as well as a member of Interpretation Canada's board.

Calvert Martin fell in love with the field of interpretation as a nature centre volunteer over 25 years ago. Since those early days, he has worked at institutions across Canada, such as Manitoba Provincial Parks, the Vancouver Aquarium, Assiniboine Park Zoo, and Metro Vancouver Regional Parks. Today, he works as a Visitor Experience Advisor for Parks Canada, runs an interpretive consultancy called Frog in the Pocket, and sits on Interpretation Canada's board as Past Chair.

André Y. Laurin discovered his passion for interpretation over 15 years ago during a cooperative education placement at a science centre when he was in high school. Having worked at an urban outreach centre, a national historic site and now as Interpretation Coordinator at Prince Edward Island National Park, André has accumulated a variety of interpretive disasters for his toolkit. A self-proclaimed naturalist-in-perpetual-training, André is a certified Heritage Interpreter and current member of Interpretation Canada's board.

About Interpretation Canada

Interpretation Canada is a community that supports, engages, and inspires those involved in the field of heritage interpretation in Canada. For more information, visit www.interpscan.ca

Love the stories in this book?

Did you immediately think, "I've got one, too!" Then, we want your story for the sequel. Please send us a short summary (just a few sentences) to stories@interpscan.ca. You may see your story in print!

www.ingramcontent.com/pod-product-compliance
Lightning Source LLC
Chambersburg PA
CBHW060056100426
42742CB00014B/2852